D1743135

Especially for

....

From

....

Date

....

The Lord's Prayer

*Devotional Prayers
Inspired by Matthew 6*

BARBOUR
PUBLISHING

© 2013 by Barbour Publishing, Inc.

Special thanks to contributing author Ellyn Sanna

Print ISBN 978-1-62416-202-2

eBook Editions:
Adobe Digital Edition (.epub) 978-1-62416-415-6
Kindle and MobiPocket Edition (.prc) 978-1-62416-414-9

All scripture quotations are taken from the King James Version
of the Bible.

Published by Barbour Publishing, Inc., P.O. Box 719,
Uhrichsville, Ohio 44683, www.barbourbooks.com

Our mission is to publish and distribute inspirational products
offering exceptional value and biblical encouragement to the masses.

Member of the
Evangelical Christian
Publishers Association

Printed in China.

CONTENTS

The *Lord's* Prayer

Our Father which art in heaven, Hallowed be thy name. Thy kingdom come, Thy will be done in earth, as it is in heaven. Give us this day our daily bread. And forgive us our debts, as we forgive our debtors. And lead us not into temptation, but deliver us from evil: For thine is the kingdom, and the power, and the glory, for ever. Amen.

MATTHEW 6:9–13

INTRODUCTION

When the disciples asked Jesus
how they should pray, He replied
with the words of what today
we know as the "Lord's Prayer."
Most of are so familiar with the
words that we may say them
automatically, forgetful of what
they actually mean. However, if
we look at these familiar phrases
more carefully, if we ponder
them and pray over them, we will
find a deeper understanding of
those things Jesus counted most
important in our relationship
with God. These are words to take
seriously and consider intimately.
They have the power to transform
our lives!

OUR FATHER IN HEAVEN

(He Is God and I Am Not)

*J*esus tells us that God is our Father: we are intimately related to the Creator of the universe. Like all good fathers, God loves us; He provides for us; He watches over us.

When we truly believe this, then we can let go of our fears for the future. Our loving Father holds all the details of our life in His hand. We don't need to worry about money. . .or health. . .or how we will handle our life's many challenges. Instead we can turn in love and trust to our Father, knowing He can do all things.

As teens, we wanted to break away from our parents, we wanted to prove our independence; this is a healthy developmental stage. But when we are spiritually mature followers of Christ, we can let God be God, and accept that He is in control.

And then we can rest in His love.

Daddy

*And because ye are sons, God hath
sent forth the Spirit of his Son into
your hearts, crying, Abba, Father.*
GALATIANS 4:6

———

Human fathers sometimes let us
down. No matter how great (or
not-so-great) my own dad is, he
is a flawed individual. But You,
Father God, always love me, always understand me, always know
what's best for me, always provide
for me, always keep Your promises. Thank You so much that
I can come to You and call You
Daddy. Help me to understand
that relationship more each day.

Everything Is Possible

Abba, Father, all things
are possible unto thee.
MARK 14:36

———◆———

How amazing, Lord—my Father is the Creator of the universe! Your infinite creativity formed the beauty of the earth and the intricacies of life. I know I can rest assured in Your strength, in Your might, in Your abilities. There's nothing in heaven or on earth that You can't handle. Forgive me when I try to take things into my own hands. Since You made the world and everything in it, I know You can take care of my small life!

Joint-Heirs with Christ

For ye have not received the spirit
of bondage again to fear; but ye
have received the Spirit of adoption,
whereby we cry, Abba, Father.
The Spirit himself bears witness
with our spirit, that we are the
children of God: And if children,
then heirs; heirs of God, and
joint-heirs with Christ.
ROMANS 8:15–17

Thank You, Lord, for adopting me into Your family, for making me Your heir, just as Jesus is. There's nothing I can do to deserve this favor or this acceptance. Your grace is all-sufficient. I now call Jesus my brother, and together we share in Your amazing glory!

Receiving Jesus

But as many as received him,
to them gave he power to become
the sons of God, even to them
that believe on his name.

JOHN 1:12

———

Lord, I believe in Your name. Help me every day to believe still more. Take away the doubts and insecurities that the world shouts at me every day. Keep my eyes firmly focused on You, even when troubles come. Keep my ears attuned to Your voice, especially when I am tempted to listen to other voices. I welcome You into my heart— to make a home there now and forever.

The Lord Almighty

And [I] will be a Father unto you, and ye shall be my sons and daughters, saith the Lord Almighty.
2 CORINTHIANS 6:18

You, God, can do all things, for You are almighty, all-powerful. Because You are my Father, I know I can trust You to handle each and every aspect of my life. Show me new ways that I can rely on You to work in a mighty way in my life. I trust You with my past, my present, and my future. You are God, and I am not—and I am thankful that's the way it is.

A Father's Mercy

*I will be his father, and he shall
be my son: and I will not take
my mercy away from him.*
1 CHRONICLES 17:13

———•———

Thank You, Lord, that You will never take Your mercy away from me. No matter how many times I let You down, I can always count on You to pick me back up. I cannot understand this gift, but I am thankful for it, Father. Please show me ways to extend mercy to others in my life—especially those whom the world may deem as "unlovable." Because the truth is, God, I know that most days I, too, am unlovable.

God of All Comfort

*Blessed be God, . . .the Father of
mercies, and the God of all comfort.*
2 CORINTHIANS 1:3

You comfort me, Father, when my
heart aches. When everything in
my life seems to be going wrong. . .
when the world is full of violence
and disaster. . .when loss is everywhere I look. . .when hope is dying
inside me, Your comfort never fails.
Thank You for offering me that
constant care in my life. Help me
to always extend comfort, care, and
compassion to others as well—
ultimately leading them to You.

What Manner of Love

Behold, what manner of love the Father hath bestowed upon us, that we should be called the sons of God.

1 JOHN 3:1

———————

A good father protects his children; he loves his children unconditionally; he understands and forgives his children; he provides for his family; he is intimately involved in the lives of those he loves. You are more than a good Father, God— You are the *perfect* Father. Remind me, Lord, that *this* is the way You love me. Thank You for loving all of me—unconditionally and without reservation.

Lights

That ye may be blameless and harmless, the sons of God, without rebuke, in the midst of a crooked and perverse nation, among whom ye shine as lights in the world.
PHILIPPIANS 2:15

Lord, I am grateful that I can claim You as my Father. Because You live in my heart, I am Your representative to the world around me. Thank You for using me for Your purpose, and thank You for filling in the gaps where I am inadequate to do Your work. Make me Your light in the world around me, not so I can gain fame for myself but only to proclaim Your awesomeness.

Children of the Resurrection

Neither can they die any more:
for they are. . .the children of God,
being the children of the resurrection.
LUKE 20:36

Because I am Your child, I don't
need to be afraid of death. You
Yourself conquered death and the
grave on Easter morning, and You
promise me that Your grace will
save me from eternal death as well.
How amazing and wonderful and
humbling! I am so glad, Lord, for
the promise of Your resurrection
and the assurance of eternity with
You in heaven. Help me to be bold
in sharing this wonderful hope
with people who have no hope.

Peace

Grace unto you, and peace,
from God our Father.
2 THESSALONIANS 1:2

———————

Thank You, Father, for the gift of Your peace. Help me to remember that Your peace is the only true and lasting rest for my soul—and to always run to You and no other idol in my life. When troubles come my way, please give me an extra dose of Your peace. And when I see others in turmoil, help me to always be ready with a word and an action that will help them seek out Your peace.

Spirit-Led

For as many as are led by the Spirit
of God, they are the sons of God.
ROMANS 8:14

———

Father, let Your Spirit lead me in each thing. Let me always look to You for guidance and direction. Keep me away from the temptation of following the paths of other "gods." Make Your Spirit alive and active in my heart, so that I might hear Your voice every day, in my every decision, and in my every action. Forgive me when I ignore the movement of Your Spirit. Make Him active in my heart, Lord!

Peacemakers

Blessed are the peacemakers: for they shall be called the children of God.
MATTHEW 5:9

——— ———

Dear Lord, teach me that if I want the world to see me as Your child, then I need to always work for peace in the world around me. Help me to resist the temptation to stir up bitterness or anger among my family, friends, and neighbors. Take away angry, jabbing words that may well up in the heat of the moment. Instead, teach me to be a peacemaker—so that others can't help but acknowledge that You are living and active within me.

Loving Our Enemies

But love ye your enemies,
and do good, and lend, hoping for
nothing again; and your reward
shall be great, and ye shall be the
children of the Highest.
LUKE 6:35

———

Heavenly Father, You know I have a hard time loving some of the people in my life. Some of them are downright nasty to me. But Your Word says that You want me to repay evil for good. Remind me that You ask me as Your child to not only love my enemies but to also do them positive, active good, without thought of reward. It's not going to be easy, Lord, but with Your help, I can do it.

God's Offspring

For in him we live, and move,
and have our being. . . .
For we are also his offspring.
ACTS 17:28

———

The world tells me to be independent, self-sufficient, and to stand on my own two feet. But the truth is that I am intimately connected to the Lord of the universe, and I rely on You for my life, Father. Most days it's a relief that it's not all on me to handle everything. To put it another way, You and I are kinfolk, Lord! I would not exist if it were not for You.

Who Knows?

Beloved, now are we the
sons of God, and it doth not
yet appear what we shall be.
1 JOHN 3:2

———

Father, I'm grateful for being Your
child in this life. I can't even imagine what that will mean in the life
to come! Thank You for the hope
You have given to me for now and
for an unknown future. Although I
don't know all the details of what
You have in store, I am thankful I
can rest secure, knowing You have
it all under control.

HALLOWED
BE THY NAME

——— ❧ ❀ ❧ ———

*(Praise Him for
Who He Is)*

When we "hallow" something, we set it apart. We keep it holy. We consecrate it. So how do we keep God's name holy and set apart?

In ancient cultures, including the one in which Jesus lived when He was on earth, a person's name was the same as the person himself. It was the essence of that person, his complete character, all that he was.

As we ask God to live in our hearts, He becomes part of us. But at the same time, He remains transcendent. When we hallow His name, we recognize that God is neither a pet we keep on a leash nor an imaginary friend we tuck into our pocket. He is greater than we are, far beyond anything our minds can even begin to comprehend.

When we realize this, we regain a healthy sense of perspective. Our own problems are not as big as we thought they were. God is so much bigger than anything our lives hold. He is unknowable, unimaginable.

And yet He loves us. Love is the essence of His character. Love is His name.

God Is Love

God is love; and he that
dwelleth in love dwelleth
in God, and God in him.
1 JOHN 4:16

God, let me never forget that You
are love—patient, kind, not envi-
ous, not proud, not rude, not self-
seeking, not easily angered, You
keep no record of wrong. You do
not delight in evil, but You rejoice
in the truth. You always protect,
trust, hope, and persevere. Your
love will always remain. It is the
greatest thing there is. May I always make my home within You—
within Your love.

Wisdom and Might

*Blessed be the name of
God for ever and ever: for
wisdom and might are his.*
DANIEL 2:20

You, Lord, are all-wise. You make the wisdom of the world look like nothing but foolishness. I will never fully grasp the vastness of Your wisdom, but I am thankful to have that strength in my corner. Scripture says that along with being all-wise, You're all-powerful as well. Speak, and the heavens and the earth are at Your beck and call. No matter how powerful we humans think we are, You are the One who holds it all. Today I "hallow Your name" by relying on Your wisdom and might.

The God of Hosts

*For, lo, he that formeth the
mountains, and createth the wind,
and declareth unto man what is his
thought, that maketh the morning
darkness, and treadeth upon the
high places of the earth, The LORD,
The God of hosts, is his name.*

AMOS 4:13

———

God, my Father, You formed the
mountains and the wind, the dark
of nighttime and the morning's
light, and You lead all the hosts of
heaven. You formed my intricate
features inside my mother's womb.
Let me never take for granted Your
limitless creativity. Let me never
forget who You truly are.

Magnifying Glasses

O magnify the LORD with me,
and let us exalt his name together.
PSALM 34:3

———————

Remind me, Father God, that I am called to be Your magnifying glass. Shine Your light through me to the all the world around me. Move me out of the way so that it's all You that others see. My aim is to exalt Your name in everything I do— in thought, word, and deed. Lead me to other people who are like-minded so that we can truly live lives that worship You and only You.

Our Redeemer

As for our redeemer,
the LORD of hosts is his name,
the Holy One of Israel.
ISAIAH 47:4

———

You are my Redeemer, Lord—You have saved me from all that separated me from You. When I am not holy, You are. When I am trapped in anxiety and despair, You free me. When I see no hope of escape from my present circumstance, You rescue me. When I feel unworthy and stained beyond all hope of saving, You cover me with grace. I worship Your name, Your presence, Your beauty, and Your strength.

The God of Our Salvation

Help us, O God of our salvation,
for the glory of thy name:
and deliver us, and purge away
our sins, for thy name's sake.

PSALM 79:9

When I start to look to other things for my salvation—money, prestige, people, possessions—remind me, God, that You are the only One who can save me now and keep me safe forever. Remove the temptations from my life that I am so quick to turn to when I'm stressed and insecure. Make me aware of the pitfalls that surround me. Focus my attention on You and Your kingdom.

The Glory of His Name

*Give unto the LORD the glory due
unto his name: bring an offering,
and come into his courts.*
PSALM 96:8

———

Lord, fill me with the glory of Your
name. May I see the splendor and
light of Your character everywhere
I turn. When I am burdened, show
me evidence of Your love in my
daily interactions with others and
with Your creation. I want to always be ready with God-filled re-
sponses to people who ask about
my hope.

Get Out of Jail Free

Whosoever shall call on the name
of the LORD shall be delivered.
JOEL 2:32

———————

Father, the world tells me there's
no such thing as a free pass. I need
to pay my dues, and then some-
day I may (if I'm lucky) reap the
reward. And of course my actions
have consequences—the world
is quick to remind me of this as
well. But, Father, when I am in
trouble—when my soul is in
captivity—remind me that all I
have to do is call Your name. . .
and You will set me free.

Majesty and Strength

*And he shall stand and feed in the
strength of the LORD, in the majesty
of the name of the LORD his God.*
MICAH 5:4

━━━━━●━━━━━

Lord, I admit that the stress of life
and the burdens of this world often
leave me feeling weak and powerless. But Your name is majesty
and strength. Your name is higher,
more powerful, and far more excel-
lent than anything this world has
to offer me. All I need to do is tap
into the power of Your name, and
You promise to sustain me. I can
do all things through You because
You give me strength!

Singing God's Name

*I will praise the name of God
with a song, and will magnify
him with thanksgiving.*
PSALM 69:30

God, fill me with Your song today. Orchestrate within my heart a melody that is truly a joyful noise, one that will bring gladness to Your heart. Give me words of praise to You and words of encouragement for others. Fill my song with Your peace and Your beauty. Help me to live out that song every moment, regardless of my circumstances. May I hallow Your name with singing.

A God of Justice

For I the LORD love judgment,
I hate robbery.
ISAIAH 61:8

If I hallow Your name, God, then I need to remember just who You really are: a God of justice. Remind me that You have called me to show the same justice in everything I do. Thank You for being the perfect balance of justice and mercy, of fairness and love. Try as I might, I cannot strike that balance in my life without Your help. Teach me to love justice and strive for justice every day.

Called by His Name

Thy words were found, and I
did eat them; and thy word was
unto me the joy and rejoicing of
mine heart: for I am called by thy
name, O LORD God of hosts.
JEREMIAH 15:16

Oh God, not only have You adopted me as Your child, but now You say I also have Your name as my own. You pursued me, You purchased me, You accepted me, You love me. Although I don't deserve the honor of being called Yours, I am so happy to accept the gift. Help me to strive to be worthy of it.

Eating God's Holiness

*That we might be
partakers of his holiness.*
HEBREWS 12:10

Father, I honor Your name by taking my fill each day of Your holiness. Make Your Spirit alive and active in my heart today. Remind me to always seek You through prayer, meditation on Your Word, and simply being still in Your presence. And when I get "too busy" to take the time to spend with You, please invite me back into Your presence. I can't handle life on my own. . .nor do I want to.

Light

*God is light, and in him
is no darkness at all.*

1 JOHN 1:5

———

Father God, Your name is light. You have no darkness in Your character. Your brilliance is dazzling— brighter than the brightest star and more beautiful than the most awe-inspiring celestial display. You are a hope-filled promise of never-ending illumination. Please shine on me—and shine *through* me so that others may see the darkness of this world flee before Your light.

The Rock

*The LORD is my rock, and my
fortress, and my deliverer; my God,
my strength, in whom I will trust;
my buckler, and the horn of my
salvation, and my high tower.*
PSALM 18:2

———◆———

So many names You have, Lord:
rock, fortress, deliverer, buckler,
horn of salvation, high tower. All
of them tell me that I can trust
You absolutely. All of them tell
me You are in control, that You
will shield me from danger, that
I shouldn't be afraid, that I am
safe in Your mighty hand. You will
never let me down.

Truth

Lead me in thy truth, and teach me:
for thou art the God of my salvation;
on thee do I wait all the day.
PSALM 25:5

———

Your Son said He was the way, the truth, and the life. Father, may I always walk in Your truth, the truth of Jesus. Teach me patience as I wait for You to move, to act in my life, as I wait for Your return. Waiting is not an easy thing to do, God. Please give me the strength to trust in the hope of my salvation in You. Your truth means everything to me.

YOUR KINGDOM COME, YOUR WILL BE DONE

(Supporting His Plans)

God's kingdom is already present. Jesus brought to earth God's saving rule; it is alive and real. But at the same time, there is much work still to be done. Peace and justice must embrace. God's saving power must heal and redeem our broken world.

When we pray that God's kingdom come and His will be done, we are aligning ourselves with God's ultimate plan for our individual lives, as well as for our world as a whole. We are accepting Christ's agenda as our own. We are celebrating God's ultimate triumph, as we look eagerly toward the day when our eyes will see His glory revealed everywhere.

Out of Sight

And when he was demanded of the Pharisees, when the kingdom of God should come, he answered them and said, The kingdom of God cometh not with observation.

LUKE 17:20

———

Father, I can't always see the reality of Your kingdom in the world around me. Give me eyes of faith. Show me the people who are working for Your goals, and give me opportunity to serve alongside them. Allow me to bring Your kingdom to the people and places around me that need You most.

Good News

He went throughout every city and village, preaching and shewing the glad tidings of the kingdom of God.
LUKE 8:1

Make me Your ambassador, Lord, carrying the good news of Your kingdom to everyone I meet today. Give me new opportunities and new relationships that I may not normally notice, so I can reach more hearts for You. Help me to see these individuals through Your eyes, as loved children of God, created in Your image. Give me the right words to say, and open their ears so they can truly understand the glad tidings of Your kingdom.

Righteousness, Peace, and Joy

For the kingdom of God is not meat and drink; but righteousness, and peace, and joy in the Holy Ghost.
ROMANS 14:17

Remind me, Father, (because I forget so easily) that Your kingdom is not built on the things of this world. The truth is that Your kingdom flies in the face of the things of the world. Righteousness, peace, and joy are heavenly attributes that we humans have a difficult time living out, without Your Spirit to change our hearts. May I not depend on external reality for my satisfaction but instead dwell always in Your realm of peace and joy.

The Sower

*And he said, So is the kingdom
of God, as if a man should
cast seed into the ground.*
MARK 4:26

———

God, what does this mean: Your
kingdom is like a man casting seed
on the ground? Does this mean
I can find Your kingdom everywhere, scattered throughout our
world by Your generous hand?
Give me new eyes to see Your
kingdom all around me, especially
in places I wouldn't expect to see
You. Father, thank You for Your
generosity. Thank You that You do
not ever withhold Yourself but are
always giving.

A Mustard Seed

The kingdom of God. . .is like
a grain of mustard seed, which,
when it is sown in the earth, is less
than all the seeds that be in the earth.
MARK 4:30–31

———

Lord, in order for Your kingdom
to grow and expand, please plant
a seed of faith in my heart. Make
my heart a fertile place for that
faith to grow so that my work in
Your kingdom will be fruitful.
Embolden Your Spirit in me so
that I might contribute greatly to
Your plans—not for my glory but
for Yours alone, Father.

Like a Child

Verily I say unto you,
Whosoever shall not receive the
kingdom of God as a little child,
he shall not enter therein.

MARK 10:15

———◆———

Give me a child's heart, Lord. Create in me the simple and heartfelt belief that You celebrate and cherish in Your children. Let me experience the wonder of Your love and gift of grace. Help me to share with others, with childlike exuberance, the hope I have in You. Let me set aside grown-up worries and live a joyful life, so that I can enter Your kingdom.

More Than Just Talk

*For the kingdom of God is
not in word, but in power.*
1 CORINTHIANS 4:20

God, sometimes I talk a good game, but my heart and actions don't carry it through. Remind me that Your kingdom is active and powerful. It's not just a bunch of talk. It's real and it's here on earth now. You ask me to help build Your kingdom; show me new ways to serve. Give me a passion for Your kingdom on earth—and for Your heavenly kingdom as well.

Blessed Poverty

Blessed be ye poor: for yours
is the kingdom of God.
LUKE 6:20

Lord, make me willing to be poor in this world so that I can be rich in Your kingdom. Give me a spirit of generosity, even giving beyond my comfort level so that I must sacrifice my feelings of security. The things of earth are not the important things, God. I know You will take care of me, and You promise me an even greater reward in heaven.

Dead and Gone

Jesus said unto him, Let the dead bury their dead: but go thou and preach the kingdom of God.
LUKE 9:60

———————

God, help me to let go of the past and look instead to Your future. I know that You hold my past, present, and future in Your hand. I give You all three, and I ask You to be my Savior that covers my past sin, lead me in Your will in my present circumstance, and be with me as I move into Your future. May I not be preoccupied with that which is dead and gone; fill my thoughts and conversation with the reality of Your kingdom in the here and now.

Healing

And heal the sick that are therein,
and say unto them, The kingdom
of God is come nigh unto you.
LUKE 10:9

———— ◦ ————

Your kingdom, Lord, brings healing to those who are sick in spirit, mind, or body. Enable me to carry Your healing to those around me. Keep me accountable; remind me to not just *say* that I will pray for others who are sick but to earnestly and intentionally come to You on their behalf. Help me to see the healing miracles You supply every moment of every day. And remind me to point others to Your goodness in those situations.

Sanctification

For this is the will of God,
even your sanctification.
1 THESSALONIANS 4:3

God, ruler of my life, You want me to be sanctified—wholly, utterly given to You. I surrender myself to Your will. I give You my heart, my family relationships, my friend relationships, my career, my ministry, my hobbies, my health. Gently prod me along to continue to surrender every area of my life to You—especially the ones that I try so desperately to take back and control on my own.

Thanks

In every thing give thanks:
for this is the will of God.
1 THESSALONIANS 5:18

———————

King of the Universe, I give You thanks for all You have given me, every moment of the day. Thanks for the health You've granted that allows me to wake up feeling alert and refreshed. Thank You for the food that nourishes my body to do Your work. Thank You for the clothes You have provided to keep me warm. Thank You for work to do so I may glorify You. Continue to fill my heart with gratitude so that I may do Your will in the world.

Delight

I delight to do thy will,
O my God.
PSALM 40:8

―――

Thank You, God, that Your will is not one of sadness and gloom. I am grateful that You are not a god that relishes seeing Your children suffer. In fact, You take great pleasure in giving good gifts to me! What a joy to know that You think of me in that way! As I learn to live always within Your kingdom, I am delighted to be able to give back in some small way as I serve You and others.

Forever

*And the world passeth away, and
the will thereof: but he that doeth
the will of God abideth for ever.*
I JOHN 2:17

The things of this world never
last. I don't know why I get ex-
cited about acquiring more and
more stuff. The anticipation is
better than the real thing, which
always ends in disappointment.
Even my cravings for this world's
things come and go. Thank You,
Lord God, that Your kingdom is
permanent, and I will dwell there
forever. Give me a passion for
eternity with You—payoff that
absolutely will not disappoint!

First Things First

But seek ye first the kingdom of God, and his righteousness; and all these things shall be added unto you.
MATTHEW 6:33

———

You understand, Lord, that I have bills to pay, deadlines to meet, a house to clean, a family to care for. These things are important, but they don't have ultimate importance. Remind me always to seek Your kingdom ahead of all these things. Give me a life of balance that is faithfully committed to Your call. Help me to trust that You will take care of (and bless) the details of my life.

Patience

For ye have need of patience, that,
after ye have done the will of God,
ye might receive the promise.
HEBREWS 10:36

———

King of my Heart, I want to do Your will. You know that sometimes, though, I grow impatient and filled with doubt. I am distracted by the temptations of the world—money, relationships, power, prestige—that look like answers to my problems. In my heart of hearts, I know they will only lead to ruin. Help me to keep going, relying on You. I know You always keep Your promises.

GIVE US TODAY OUR DAILY BREAD

(Supply My Needs)

*I*t's a human tendency to try to safeguard the future. We feel more in control if we think we can guarantee that we'll have everything we'll need down the road. There's nothing wrong with insurance policies or savings accounts, but ultimately, none of us can control what the future holds.

In Jesus' prayer, He speaks of "daily bread," not weekly, not monthly, not yearly. Just as God sent the Israelites manna to collect each morning—food that spoiled when they tried to stockpile it for the next day—God promises to give us exactly what we need for the day ahead. Day by day, He meets our needs for physical and spiritual food.

God wants us to depend only on Him, each day of our lives, believing that He will give us exactly what we need.

That's what it means to walk by faith.

Enough

God is able to make all grace abound
toward you; that ye, always having
all sufficiency in all things, may
abound to every good work.
2 CORINTHIANS 9:8

———

You make me sufficient, Lord—
You give me enough of everything
I need—to carry out Your will.
Truth be told, You often supply
much more than I need. These bless-
ings are wonderful surprises that
I don't want to take for granted.
Show me ways that I can share
Your blessings with others. You are
a good giver, Lord. Thank You.

God's Riches

My God shall supply all your
need according to his riches
in glory by Christ Jesus.
PHILIPPIANS 4:19

Why should I ever doubt Your ability to give me what I need, heavenly Father, when You have such riches? Your bounty is unfathomable, and You want to share it with me! How humbling! Help me to remember that everything I call "mine" is actually Yours. Forgive me when my heart is hard and unwilling to accept Your riches in glory. Help me to be open to Your Spirit as He moves in my heart.

No Wants

The LORD is my shepherd;
I shall not want.
PSALM 23:1

———— ◆ ————

Since You are looking out for me—guarding and guiding me—I have everything I need. You are the Good Shepherd who supplies everything to me, Your sheep. Remind me every day that as a sheep, I cannot see the bigger picture—the dangers over the hill or the blessings that are mine to find. Help me to more fully trust the Shepherd and His plans for me. Give me a heart of gratitude and a spirit that relinquishes control. Thank You, Lord.

Seed and Bread

Now he that ministereth seed
to the sower both minister bread
for your food, and multiply
your seed sown, and increase the
fruits of your righteousness.
2 CORINTHIANS 9:10

God, You aren't just a sower or a harvester; You're a true farmer. First You plant the seed; then You water it and nurture it, giving me the food and encouragement I need to grow in You. You work tirelessly to reap a bountiful harvest when my heart is full of fertile soil. I want to return the harvest to You, bearing beautiful fruits of righteousness. Keep working on me, farmer God—I am willing.

Like Birds

*Consider the ravens: for they
neither sow nor reap; which neither
have storehouse nor barn; and God
feedeth them: how much more are
ye better than the fowls?*

LUKE 12:24

———

Lord, if You keep track of the lives
of birds, then I know I can trust
You to watch over my own life.
May I rest in the knowledge that
You are always looking after me.
I know I am worth much more to
You than a bird. And even though I
know I don't deserve it, I thank You
for Your unconditional love.

Priorities

*Therefore I say unto you, Take no
thought for your life, what ye shall
eat, or what ye shall drink; nor yet
for your body, what ye shall put on.
Is not the life more than meat,
and the body than raiment?*

MATTHEW 6:25

———

When I start to worry over little
things, help me to keep my priori-
ties in order, Father God. Give me
grace not to make mountains out
of molehills. Time and time again,
You have proven that You are faithful to take care of me, so what right
do I have to worry? Keep my heart
steadfast and my footing secure in
the knowledge that You hold me in
Your hand.

Prayer and Thanksgiving

*Be careful for nothing; but in every
thing by prayer and supplication
with thanksgiving let your requests
be made known unto God.*

PHILIPPIANS 4:6

———

Even while I'm asking You for
something, Lord, I can already
thank You. I know You hear my
prayers, and will answer with "Yes,"
"No," or "Wait." Thank You for often taking care of my needs even
before I ask. What a comfort it
is that You already know what I
need. I can trust You absolutely to
answer me in the best way and according to Your purpose.

God's Ears

And if we know that he hear us,
whatsoever we ask, we know
that we have the petitions
that we desired of him.
1 JOHN 5:15

———————

Thank You, God, that You are always listening to me. You never ignore my prayers, no matter how silly or insignificant I think my words might be. It's a mystery how You can possibly hear the requests of all of mankind at the same time, but You do! And each moment of communication is important to You. Thank You for being a God with always-listening ears.

Promises

Whatsoever we ask, we receive
of him, because we keep his
commandments, and do those things
that are pleasing in his sight.
1 JOHN 3:22

———◆———

Help me to keep Your commandments and always live in a way that pleases You, my Lord. I know Your commandments are not meant to be a burden to me but to keep me safe from harm, from temptations, and to allow me to live in the freedom of Your love. Forgive me for the times I feel that Your laws are constraining to me.

Persistence!

Ask, and it shall be given you;
seek, and ye shall find; knock,
and it shall be opened unto you.
MATTHEW 7:7

———————

May I trust You enough, Lord, to ask You for what I need—and then to keep asking, seeking, and knocking, until You answer. Help me not to grow weary in coming to You in prayer. I know that You will keep Your promises—that You hear me and are working in the details of my life. When I am praying for others, keep me committed to taking them to You.

Confidence

Therefore I say unto you,
What things soever ye desire, when
ye pray, believe that ye receive them,
and ye shall have them.
MARK 11:24

———————

Thank You, Father, that I can come to You in confidence. I am so unworthy to be able to be given access to You through prayer, yet You delight in the communication we have. When I bring requests to You, I want those requests to be things that are not selfish or outside of Your will. Grant that my desires are Your desires, Father. I know that You will always give me whatever I truly need.

Tomorrow

Take therefore no thought for the morrow: for the morrow shall take thought for the things of itself.
MATTHEW 6:34

The truth is that I have no control over tomorrow, Lord. Free me from worries about the future, whether tomorrow or next week or next year. May I rely on You today, so that I can focus on the here and now, this moment, and trust You to take care of whatever comes next. I do trust You, Father. Help my actions be evidence to that fact. I yearn for the freedom that comes from being worry-free!

Heart's Desire

*Delight thyself also in the LORD:
and he shall give thee the
desires of thine heart.*
PSALM 37:4

━━━━━◆━━━━━

Thank You, God, that You created the deepest, truest desires that live within me. You have made me uniquely different from everyone else, and You've given me a desire to live inside Your will. Thank You for the passions and gifts You have given me. Please show me ways that I can use those gifts to be a blessing to You. I'm glad that as I delight in You, I can trust You always to meet the needs of my yearning heart.

Open Up Wide!

*I am the LORD thy God,
which brought thee out of
the land of Egypt: open thy
mouth wide, and I will fill it.*
PSALM 81:10

———

Lord, like a baby bird, I will open
wide my soul's mouth, knowing
that You will always feed me all
I need. Open up my heart today,
God, and fill it to the brim with
just what I need: encouragement,
joy, a spirit of servanthood, a passion for the lost, patience, kindness,
and a love for others. I'm ready,
Father—fill me up!

Satisfied

And the LORD shall guide thee
continually, and satisfy thy soul
in drought, and make fat thy bones:
and thou shalt be like a watered
garden, and like a spring of water,
whose waters fail not.
ISAIAH 58:11

Even in the midst of everyday life's droughts—when everything seems dry and dead and dusty—thank You, Father, that You continue to water my heart and satisfy soul. When I see others are in the midst of drought, give me the right words and actions to share Your living water that will keep them from ever being thirsty again.

Hungry Souls

For he satisfieth the longing soul, and filleth the hungry soul with goodness.
PSALM 107:9

———— ◆ ————

God, my soul gets so hungry for You sometimes. I know that it's not You that has moved away, but the problem is with me. Thank You that You are immovable, unshakable, and always there. Because of this, I know just where to run to find You, to satisfy my longing soul. Give me a firm footing in Your presence so I am not tempted to wander away again. Thank You for being patient with me.

FORGIVE US OUR DEBTS

(Cleanse My Sins)

Sin is what separates us from God. It is everything that is broken, everything that goes off course, away from the path that God wants for our lives. Our hearts are naturally inclined to go astray. And when they do, we feel soiled. . . lost. . .poverty-struck. . .miserable . . .ashamed.

But Jesus came to take away those feelings. He came to get us back on track. He is the bridge that spans the divide that sin makes between God and our hearts. No matter how many times we swerve off course, He's always ready to reach out His hand and pull us back.

Rich in Grace

In whom we have redemption
through his blood, the forgiveness
of sins, according to the riches
of his grace...
EPHESIANS 1:7

The world tells me I should be rich
in material wealth, Father, but true
riches are found in Your limitless
grace. Thank You for the richness
of Your grace, Lord. Thank You
that Your grace is large enough
to cover all my past sin, my cur-
rent sin, and my future sin. That's
the kind of rich inheritance I truly
desire!

Promises

*This is my blood of the new
testament, which is shed for
many for the remission of sins.*
MATTHEW 26:28

Jesus' blood is the new testament—
the new promise You have made to
me, Lord. I am not bound by the
rules and regulations of the Old
Testament law, but instead I have
been given amazing freedom! The
blood of Jesus is so powerful that
I cannot comprehend it, but please
help me to always rely on His saving blood that heals all my sins.

Faithful

If we confess our sins, he is faithful and just to forgive us our sins, and to cleanse us from all unrighteousness.

1 JOHN 1:9

———

God, I confess to You that I have sinned. I have gone astray, away from Your love. Again and again I fall short. It shames to me admit it, but You ask for my confession. Forgive me. Wash me. Bring me home. Thank You that even now, I can rely on Your faithful love. Thank You for the promise that You are faithful to forgive me—not just yesterday and today, but tomorrow as well.

Power

*The Son of man hath power
on earth to forgive sins.*
MARK 2:10

Jesus, no one else has the power to forgive sins like You do. You took the shame of my sins on Your shoulders as You hung on the cross. I cannot understand the immense pain and suffering You endured as You were beaten and ridiculed. You paid for me. You took care of my insurmountable debt. Thank You for Your sacrifice, and thank You for Your power that sets me free from my sins.

God's Name

Help us, O God of our salvation,
for the glory of thy name:
and deliver us, and purge away
our sins, for thy name's sake.
PSALM 79:9

I know that my sins make me dirty, God. More than that, my sins separate me from You. But because You are who You are, You make me clean, Lord. You cover me in the blood of the Lamb, and You deliver me from all my sin so that I may dwell in Your presence. It's nothing that I've done on my own. May I always bring Your name glory!

Purged

Iniquities prevail against me:
as for our transgressions,
thou shalt purge them away.
PSALM 65:3

———— • ————

I mess up a lot, Father. In fact, sin seems stronger than me sometimes, dear Lord. It takes such a steady foothold in my life that I feel powerless to change. Purge away this tendency from my heart, I pray. I will focus on You and Your Word, Savior God, and I know that You will lead me away from the temptation of sin.

Backsliding

*O LORD, though our iniquities
testify against us, do thou it for
thy name's sake: for our backslidings
are many; we have sinned against
thee. . . .thou, O LORD, art in the
midst of us, and we are called by
thy name; leave us not.*
JEREMIAH 14:7, 9

No matter how far along I go in
my spiritual walk with You, Lord,
sooner or later I always start to
slide backward. There are some
temptations and situations that will
always make me struggle, and I admit that sometimes I succumb to
those temptations and sin. And yet
You are here with me. Don't leave
me now.

Rebellion

*To the Lord our God belong
mercies and forgivenesses, though
we have rebelled against him.*
DANIEL 9:9

Sometimes I act like a two-year-old
or a teenager—I want to do what I
want to do when I want to do it. I
disregard what I know is right and
good and travel down a dangerous
path. Even when I'm in the middle
of the situation, I know I'm doing
wrong. I rebel against Your love,
Lord. Thank You that despite my
sheer stupidity, You always forgive
me, even though I don't deserve it.
Help me never to take advantage
of Your forgiveness.

Merciful

I will be merciful to their
unrighteousness, and their
sins and their iniquities will
I remember no more.
HEBREWS 8:12

Thank You that You are a merciful God. You don't even remember all the many times I let You
down! You truly forgive and forget.
Teach me how to show this kind
of mercy to people in my life who
have wronged me—that I may
shine Your light to others in a real
and genuine way, with unconditional love.

Delighted in Mercy

Who is a God like unto thee,
that pardoneth iniquity, and
passeth by the transgression of
the remnant of his heritage? he
retaineth not his anger for ever,
because he delighteth in mercy.
MICAH 7:18

————————

Father, sometimes when I seek Your forgiveness for a sin that I commit over and over again, I assume that while You are still forgiving me, You might be doing so begrudgingly. But the truth is that You delight in mercy! So You delight in forgiving me? What an amazing thought! What would I do without Your mercy?

Blotted Out

*I, even I, am he that blotteth out thy
transgressions for mine own sake,
and will not remember thy sins.*
ISAIAH 43:25

———

God, I'm so thankful that You don't
hold grudges. I give You thanks
and praise, dear Lord, for You have
not only wiped away all my sins
but You also don't even remember
them! You wipe my slate clean; You
give me a new start; You hit the
RESET button. You have made me
truly free from the past.

Insurmountable Distance

As far as the east is from the west, so far hath he removed our transgressions from us.
PSALM 103:12

———————

Whenever I feel that I'm a hopeless case, that I'll never be able to rise above the sin that I fall into, remind me, Father, that from Your perspective, my soul and my sin might as well be in different dimensions, separated by an insurmountable distance. Take away my shame and guilt that I feel about my past sins, and help me to rest in the fact that I am completely forgiven.

Behind God's Back

*Thou hast in love to my soul
delivered it from the pit of
corruption: for thou hast cast
all my sins behind thy back.*

ISAIAH 38:17

I have to imagine that if You put
something behind Your back, Creator God, it doesn't really even exist
anymore. You don't want to look at
it, think about it, or even be both-
ered by it. Always remind me that
this is what You have done with my
sins! I am free!

The Depths of the Sea

*He will have compassion upon
us; he will subdue our iniquities;
and thou wilt cast all their sins
into the depths of the sea.*
MICAH 7:19

Thank You for Your loving compassion, heavenly Father, that throws my sin to the bottom of the darkest, deepest ocean—never to be thought of again. Take all the selfish urges of my heart and subdue them, so that I may be free to serve You as I long to.

New Clothes

Take away the filthy garments
from him. And unto him he said,
Behold, I have caused thine iniquity
to pass from thee, and I will clothe
thee with change of raiment.
ZECHARIAH 3:4

———◆———

Lord, You offer me a brand-new wardrobe to replace my filthy clothes that are stained with sin. Forgive me when I wrongfully believe that my dirty rags are adequate and I try to hold on to them. Help me to put on the new clothes You hold out to me. Dress me in Your love and forgiveness.

Showered

Then will I sprinkle clean water
upon you, and ye shall be clean:
from all your filthiness, and from
all your idols, will I cleanse you.
EZEKIEL 36:25

Each time I take a shower, God, remind me that You have showered my soul with Your love. As I lather up with soap that will cleanse the dirt of the day, remind me of the cleansing power of Your grace and mercy. You have washed away everything in me that was false, and now I am truly clean.

AS WE ALSO HAVE FORGIVEN OUR DEBTORS

———— ⚜ ❀ ⚜ ————

(Teach Me to Forgive)

When someone treats us in a way that seems unfair, we so easily focus on that slight. We brood over it. We talk to others about it. It keeps us awake at night. Even the smallest offenses can grow larger and larger in our minds, the more we think about them. And when it comes to truly large offenses—when someone has hurt a person we love, for example, or when violence is done to innocents in the world—we feel justified in seething in anger and outrage.

But this isn't what forgiveness looks like. Forgiveness sets aside slights, no matter how real or undeserved or huge they may be. Forgiveness imitates the mercy God has shown to our own hearts. It remembers that when God has forgiven us of so much, we can afford to forgive others as well.

Jesus asks us to forgive.

Whenever I Pray

And when ye stand praying, forgive,
if ye have ought against any: that
your Father also which is in heaven
may forgive you your trespasses.
MARK 11:25

———————

Whenever I come to You, Lord,
asking You to grant me some request, remind me first to let go
of any unforgiveness I'm holding
in my heart. I don't want to be a
grudge-holder, and I know that
withholding forgiveness hurts me
more than it hurts the other person. Show me ways to show true
grace—Your grace—to others who
have hurt me.

Anger Deferred

The word *glory* refers to the essence of something, the quality that makes it give forth light. Dear God, remind me that I am most truly myself, my best and shiniest self, when I don't act on my anger against others. Give me the wisdom to know how to react to people and situations in the same way You would react. Let love, respect, and kindness be at the root of everything I do.

Persecution

———

Father, bless all those who have hurt me, all those who have hurt those I love, all those who have hurt the innocents of our world. I ask that You show me how to reach out my hands in kind and practical ways to these individuals who have brought hurt into our world. Help me to see past their actions to their own hurt. Use me to show them Your mercy and love.

Blessings Instead of Curses

Bless them that curse you, and pray for them which despitefully use you.
LUKE 6:28

My Lord, I feel misused. I feel cursed. I feel slighted and abused. I'm angry and hurt. I come to You with these feelings, and I give them to You. Take away the hurt and my desire for revenge. Give me Your heart when it comes to others. I pray that You would bless the people who have made me feel this way. Your will be done, Father.

Inheritance of Blessing

Not rendering evil for evil, or railing
for railing: but contrariwise blessing;
knowing that ye are thereunto called,
that ye should inherit a blessing.
1 PETER 3:9

———

It's my first reaction to strike back
when I'm hurt, to complain against
people who complain about me.
You know those tendencies within
me, Father. Turn them inside out,
I pray, and may my first reaction
instead be always to pray and bless.
When I feel that this is too much
to ask of me, remind me that You
will give back to me countless
blessings in return.

Putting Up With It!

Being reviled, we bless; being persecuted, we suffer it.
1 CORINTHIANS 4:12

———◆———

God, give me patience to put up with all the grief that comes my way! You know the things that push my buttons, that get under my skin. Give me the peace to endure them. I know You will use the situation according to Your will, but it's not so fun to suffer through it! Give me the comfort and encouragement I need to endure.

Feeding My Enemies

Therefore if thine enemy hunger, feed him; if he thirst, give him drink.
ROMANS 12:20

———

It's not enough to *forgive* my enemies, Lord; now You ask me to actively do them good—to do whatever I can to meet their needs. I'm hurting so much right now that I can't do this on my own, Father. Show me how You want me to do that, and then give me the strength to do it. May I look for opportunities to help those who have hurt me.

Waiting for God

Say not thou, I will recompense
evil; but wait on the LORD,
and he shall save thee.

PROVERBS 20:22

When a situation arises where
wrong has been done, I'm quick to
feel that the situation is urgent: I
have to do something about it *right
now*. Teach me, Lord, to wait for
You instead. Give me Your wisdom in these situations, and when
the time is right, show me what to
say and what to do that will bring
glory to You.

The Other Cheek

Whosoever shall smite thee
on thy right cheek, turn
to him the other also.
MATTHEW 5:39

Really, God? If someone hurts me,
do I really have to ask him to hurt
me again somewhere else? That
seems like You're asking too much!
It goes against everything society
teaches me about standing up for
myself, about being assertive, about
not being a doormat. Teach me
what Jesus meant when He said
this. Give me a heart that wants to
follow His example. . .even when I
don't want to.

Following Good

See that none render evil for
evil unto any man; but ever follow
that which is good, both among
yourselves, and to all men.
1 Thessalonians 5:15

Even when I see evil all around me, Lord, help me to always follow that which is good rather than evil. Forgive me when I am lured by the fake shininess and beauty that evil displays. Keep me from falling for the tricks of the devil, and keep my feet securely on Your path, the good and right path.

Love

[Love] beareth all things,
believeth all things, hopeth
all things, endureth all things.
1 CORINTHIANS 13:7

———

Give me a loving heart, God. Help me to endure hurts, always hoping and believing in the best in others. Remind me that love is an everyday action, not just when I feel like it. Help me to show love in words as well. Give me Your eyes to see the true worth of the people around me, and help me to always display Your love to them. Thank You for being the perfect example of love.

Quarrels

*Forbearing one another, and
forgiving one another, if any man
have a quarrel against any: even as
Christ forgave you, so also do ye.*
COLOSSIANS 3:13

———

Quarrels come so easily some days,
Lord, especially with the people
I live and work with the most
closely. Remind me that Christ
has forgiven me for far greater
offenses, and help me to bite my
tongue before I start an argument.
When I do stumble and take part
in a fight, help me to be humble
and ask for forgiveness from the
other person. Grant me freedom
in my relationships so I am not
distracted by bitterness.

Tenderhearted

And be ye kind one to another,
tenderhearted, forgiving one
another, even as God for Christ's
sake hath forgiven you.
EPHESIANS 4:32

———

The world may look at a tender
heart as a weakness, but You know
better, God. Your heart is tender
toward me, and You are quick to
extend grace and mercy. Give me
a tender heart, I pray. Guard my
heart so that it won't become cal-
loused to the hurts and evils of the
world. Fill me with Your kindness,
gentleness, compassion, and sin-
cerity, so that I can forgive others
just as I have been forgiven.

Overcoming

Be not overcome of evil, but
overcome evil with good.
ROMANS 12:21

When darkness seems to be attacking me from all sides, Lord, give me Your strength so that I can rise above the world's evil. Make Your Spirit strong in me so that I can feel Your presence near. Give me the words to say and the things to do to bring Your goodness to every situation. Use me in whatever way You can for Your will to be done. I know I'm on the winning side!

God's Children

Be ye therefore followers
of God, as dear children.
EPHESIANS 5:1

———◆———

Brothers and sisters often bicker and squabble. My siblings and I are no exception. But remind me, dear God, that Your children should be following You, not fighting with each other. Grant us an abundance of grace when we are dealing with each other, and help us keep our eyes solely on You as we work through difficulties. If we are following Your will, we will be blessed beyond imagination.

Merciful

Be ye therefore merciful,
as your Father also is merciful.
LUKE 6:36

Father, I am so thankful for Your
mercy, and I am thankful for Your
gift of grace—but You know that
it is sometimes difficult for me to
show mercy to others. It's especially
hard for me to be merciful when I
see someone making the same mis-
take over again or committing the
same sin again and again. But right
now I pray that You make me like
You. Help me to show Your mercy
to everyone—with no exceptions.

AND LEAD US
NOT INTO
TEMPTATION

—≫❀≪—

*(Protect My Heart
and Spirit)*

As children, many of us felt confused by this verse in the Lord's Prayer; it seems to indicate that God will tempt us to sin unless we specifically ask Him not to do so. Other translations for the Greek word, however, might be "trials" or "tests."

Life brings to all of us difficult times, times when our faith and strength is tested. Jesus is telling us here in His prayer that during those times, we can ask for God's help and protection. When we are tested, God will help us to pass with flying colors. He will help us escape our times of trials.

Shielded

Above all, taking the shield of faith,
wherewith ye shall be able to quench
all the fiery darts of the wicked.
EPHESIANS 6:16

Lord, You tell me that my faith is a shield that will protect me from evil. Right now I ask You to reinforce that shield. Give me a greater, stronger faith so that I will be ready when I go through difficult times, when Satan is shooting his fiery darts directly at me. I will not live in fear about this possibility, but I will stand on Your promises.

God's Gentleness

Thou hast also given me the shield
of thy salvation: and thy gentleness
hath made me great.
2 SAMUEL 22:36

Father God, when I think about Your gift of salvation to me, I think about the mighty work that Your grace through the death of Jesus Christ does in my life. But there's another side to it. God, thank You for Your gentleness that makes me strong enough to rise above every trial that comes my way. It's because I am saved that I can be free to stand and not be afraid.

God's Armor

But let us, who are of the day,
be sober, putting on the breastplate
of faith and love; and for an helmet,
the hope of salvation.
1 THESSALONIANS 5:8

———

Father, remind me not to venture out into life's temptations and trials without first putting on Your armor, especially the breastplate of faith and love and the helmet of Your salvation. Teach me to grab hold of these gifts and harness the power that You offer through them. Give me the opportunity to use these pieces of armor to bless others, protecting them against the power of evil.

Lit

*Let your loins be girded about,
and your lights burning.*
LUKE 12:35

When everywhere I look I see only
darkness, please, Lord, turn on the
lights in my heart. Show me ways
to share that illumination with
everyone around me. When Your
light burns, darkness flees. Use me.
Light me, I pray.

Wide Awake

Therefore let us not sleep, as do others;
but let us watch and be sober.
1 THESSALONIANS 5:6

———

You know how tired I am, God. You know how weary I am of facing troubles and challenges. Help me not surrender to my exhaustion. Send godly friends into my life that can encourage me to continue on the path that You have laid for Your children. Keep me wide awake and alert, focused always on You.

Delivered

*Because he hath set his love upon
me, therefore will I deliver him:
I will set him on high, because
he hath known my name.*

PSALM 91:14

———

When troubles threaten to drown
me, loving Lord, reach down
and save me. Deliver me from
the floods. Rescue me from the
fire. Remove me from the storm.
Protect me from the violence.
Pick me up and set me on a high
place where I will be safe in Your
presence. I know my deliverer is
coming.

Preserved

The LORD preserveth
all them that love him.
PSALM 145:20

━━━◆━━━

Preserve me, God; keep me safe—
that's what I'm asking of You.
Guard my physical body, my head,
and my heart. Grant me travel
mercies as I move from place to
place. Take away my anxiety, my
worries, and my woes. I love You—
and I need Your help now. I can't
do it alone.

Alive and Blessed

The LORD will preserve him,
and keep him alive; and he shall
be blessed upon the earth: and
thou wilt not deliver him unto
the will of his enemies.

PSALM 41:2

———————

Sickness...violence...exhaustion...
stress: our world is full of dangers.
Some of the dangers I face are
truly life-threatening, Lord. But I
don't want to live a life of fear. You
call me to be bold and fearless.
Thank You that You've promised
to not only save my life but also to
bless me.

Never Forsaken

For the LORD loveth judgment,
and forsaketh not his saints;
they are preserved for ever.
PSALM 37:28

———◆———

Father God, I've experienced abandonment in my life. The experience left me feeling empty, alone, helpless. Thank You, Father, that You will never forsake me; You will never abandon me. I am grateful for the security this promise affords me. You will keep me safe forever in Your loving arms that are big enough and strong enough to hold me and all my issues.

Saved from All Evil

*The LORD shall preserve thee from
all evil: he shall preserve thy soul.*
PSALM 121:7

Evil comes in so many shapes and
forms. Sometimes it comes into
my life disguised, and by the time
I recognize its presence, my soul is
already in danger. When this hap-
pens, Father, be my rescuer (even
when I don't ask for rescuing!).
Thank You, Lord, that You are always watching over me—and You
will protect me from evil of every
kind.

My Hiding Place

Thou art my hiding place; thou
shalt preserve me from trouble;
thou shalt compass me about
with songs of deliverance.
PSALM 32:7

Heavenly Father, when the world seems like a dangerous place, when anxieties rush at me everywhere I turn, be my hiding place. Be by my side, and let me run into Your arms. Wrap me up in Your embrace, and sing to me Your sweet song of deliverance. May I never think I'm so self-sufficient that I reject Your comfort and protection, Daddy.

A Tower on a Rock

*The God of my rock; in him will
I trust: he is my shield, and the
horn of my salvation, my high
tower, and my refuge, my saviour;
thou savest me from violence.*

2 SAMUEL 22:3

———

You, oh Lord, are my place of absolute safety: a high tower built on a rock that will never move. When trials and temptations surround me, teach me to lift my gaze higher. Help me to look above all my troubles and see Your tall tower—and then run there as fast as I can!

My Refuge

The LORD also will be a
refuge for the oppressed,
a refuge in times of trouble.
PSALM 9:9

In times of trouble, Lord, when I feel that the pressure is overwhelming, thank You that You are my refuge—a place of peace, love, and acceptance. Teach me to seek Your protection at the onset of troubles, rather than trying to handle them on my own. I don't get extra points for trying to stick it out by myself.

Singing

But I will sing of thy power;
yea, I will sing aloud of thy
mercy in the morning: for thou
hast been my defence and refuge
in the day of my trouble.

PSALM 59:16

———————

God, You know all the troubles that surround me—but today, I'm going to start my day singing. Give me a song of power and mercy that will stay with me all day long, especially when the stresses of the day come. No matter what life throws at me, I want to live with Your joyful melody in my heart until Jesus returns to take me home!

Hope

*Thou art my hiding place and my
shield: I hope in thy word.*
PSALM 119:114

———⊸⊷———

God, I know that one of the surest ways to find Your hope is to open up scripture and meditate on Your Word. There I learn that You thought of me at the beginning of creation, that You formed me in my mother's womb, that You love me and cherish me, that You provided a way for me to have an intimate relationship with You through the death, burial, and resurrection of Jesus Christ, and that You have amazing plans for me here and into eternity. Your words fill me with amazing hope, Father.

Safe in the Midst of the World

I pray not that thou shouldest take them out of the world, but that thou shouldest keep them from the evil.

JOHN 17:15

Jesus, You didn't ask that I be physically removed from the earth, so that I'd be immune to the world's temptations and tests. Instead, You asked that God protect me no matter what I face. Thank You, Jesus, that You prayed for *me*.

BUT DELIVER
US FROM THE
EVIL ONE

(Guide My Steps)

*J*esus didn't pretend that there was no evil in the world. Instead, He teaches us in His prayer to focus on God's deliverance. Even when us are surrounded by evil's darkness— even when this life's evil presses so close around we that we can see nothing with our own eyesight— even then, God will guide our steps.

We may not be able to see the path ahead, but God knows the way. He will keep us safe as we continue on life's journey, through the darkest days. We may not always be able to know He is there, but He will never forsake us. And one day, He will lead us safely home.

Yes and No

But let your communication be,
Yea, yea; Nay, nay: for whatsoever
is more than these cometh of evil.
MATTHEW 5:37

God, teach me Your ways so that no evil will take root in my life. Remind me to make my word count, so that my "yes" means yes, and my "no" means no. Make me a person of integrity that others can trust. When people ask me why I do what I do, let me always point them to You.

Clothed in Truth

Stand therefore, having your loins girt about with truth, and having on the breastplate of righteousness.
EPHESIANS 6:14

Father, this world has exchanged truth for lies. What You see as black and white, society sees as gray. Right and wrong has been twisted in such a way that many people are confused and don't even know *what* to think. Today I ask that You clothe me in truth, so that I can live as You want me to. Give me the boldness to stand up for what is right, and in love guide others to You, the ultimate source of truth.

Hope to the End

Wherefore gird up the loins of your mind, be sober, and hope to the end for the grace that is to be brought unto you at the revelation of Jesus Christ.

1 PETER 1:13

———————

I have put my hope in Your grace, Lord, which You showed to me through the life of Your Son, Jesus Christ. The account of His death, burial, and resurrection is one that saves me for all of eternity, but meanwhile, I want to emulate His example of grace-filled living now, in my everyday life. Help me to always keep His example as my focus.

Firm

But the Lord is faithful, who shall stablish you, and keep you from evil.
2 THESSALONIANS 3:3

———— ————

God, I know You are faithful. Be my rock and my firm foothold, and please be the foundation of my life. Make me firm and solid, so that I can always resist evil. When my own faith is firmly rooted, then please allow me to help others find their strength in Your faithfulness. Your strength will sustain all Your children!

No Slipping

He will not suffer thy
foot to be moved: he that
keepeth thee will not slumber.
PSALM 121:3

———

I'm coming to a situation in my life where the way ahead looks slippery and dangerous, Lord. Please hold my hand, and when necessary pick me up and carry me. I know that You won't leave me or even take a break to get a little rest. Thank You that I can rest in You, even during difficult stretches of the path.

Straight Ways

Lead me, O LORD,
in thy righteousness because
of mine enemies; make thy
way straight before my face.
PSALM 5:8

———————

God, You know how hard it is for me sometimes to know which way I should go. Today I ask that You be my map and my guide. Please show me clearly the way You want me to follow. Remind me that You've already been there and done that. While I may question why we're going a certain way, You know what is best, and You have great plans for me.

Plain Paths

Teach me thy way, O LORD,
and lead me in a plain path,
because of mine enemies.
PSALM 27:11

———————

I need Your help, Lord. I can't see which path I should take. It's dark, I'm confused, and the enemy of my soul has hidden Your way from me. Please, Lord, lead me—and remove the evil that is in the way!

Walking in Truth

Teach me thy way, O LORD;
I will walk in thy truth: unite
my heart to fear thy name.
PSALM 86:11

I am guilty of having a divided heart, God. I want to do Your will, but I also want my will to be done. Forgive me for my selfishness. When my heart feels torn with conflicting desires, Father God, please unite me, so that I have a single focus in life: Your way, Your truth, Your will, Your path.

Morning Love

Cause me to hear thy lovingkindness
in the morning; for in thee do I
trust: cause me to know the way
wherein I should walk; for I lift
up my soul unto thee.
PSALM 143:8

───────────●───────────

It is my desire, Father God, to meet
You in prayer every morning. As
I start out each day, give me ears,
loving Lord, to hear Your voice—
and then may I listen for that still,
small voice all through my day.
Follow me into the evening and
whisper loving thoughts to me at
night as I rest my head, ready to
meet You again in the morning.

God's Eye

I will instruct thee and teach thee
in the way which thou shalt go:
I will guide thee with mine eye.
PSALM 32:8

———

I have a dog that follows the direction of my gaze and knows what I want her to do. All I need to do is look at her bed for her to go there and lie down; if I look in another direction, toward a treat I've hidden for her, she leaps up and runs to the morsel of food. Lord, help me to be as responsive to Your gaze. Keep me so tuned into You that You can use Your eyes to show me where You want me to go.

For My Own Good

———◆———

Sometimes I forget, Lord, that Your guidance is always for my good. I admit that sometimes it feels a little bit like taking my medicine. But You want what's truly best for me. Your paths always lead me to joy and blessing and health. Teach me to trust You more fully today and every day.

Open Ears

And thine ears shall hear a word
behind thee, saying, This is the way,
walk ye in it, when ye turn to the right
hand, and when ye turn to the left.

ISAIAH 30:21

Give me sharp ears, heavenly Father, so that I can hear Your voice. Tune my ears to be receptive to only You, and give me discernment so I can disregard the false voices that may try to imitate You.

No More Crooked Ways

*I will bring the blind by a way
that they knew not; I will lead
them in paths that they have not
known: I will make darkness light
before them, and crooked things
straight. These things will I do unto
them, and not forsake them.*

ISAIAH 42:16

―――――――

Sometimes my life's path seems to take one expected turn after another. I feel as though I'm stumbling through a dark maze. One day, though, Lord, when I look back at my life from heaven's perspective, will I see that You made my life's crooked paths run absolutely straight, right to You?

The Path of Life

*Thou wilt shew me the path
of life: in thy presence is fulness of
joy; at thy right hand there
are pleasures for evermore.*

PSALM 16:11

———

Why do I think I'm a trailblazer,
Lord? Sometimes my way seems
better to me, so I take a little side
trip off Your path, only to find
disappointment, destruction, and
heartbreak. I know that only Your
path, God, leads me to life. . .to joy
. . .to pleasures that will last forever. I will put blinders on my eyes,
Father—looking straight ahead
to You.

Standing Up Straight

Teach me to do thy will; for thou art my God: thy spirit is good; lead me into the land of uprightness.

PSALM 143:10

My burdens have been feeling extra heavy lately, Father. I am still walking along Your path, but maybe You've noticed my shoulders slumped, my head hung low. Gently remind me that I don't need to carry these burdens—that You are strong enough to carry all the weight of the world. I give You my worries and woes, Father. Help me to stand upright and follow the path of Your perfect will.

Everlasting Ways

See if there be any wicked way in me,
and lead me in the way everlasting.
PSALM 139:24

You know, Lord God, how easily
I hide selfishness inside my heart.
But try as I might, I cannot hide
it from You. Shine Your light on
all my blind spots. Show me where
I need to grow and change to be
more like You. Bring true godly
friends into my life that can help
me in these areas. Lead me in the
path that will lead me to eternity.

FOR YOURS IS THE KINGDOM AND THE POWER AND THE GLORY FOREVER

(Prayers for My Future)

We look forward to the future if we think we can predict that it will hold good things, but we dread and fear the difficult things we know lie ahead. We cannot escape death and old age, loss and sorrow. And we fear the unknown, the future we can't predict or control.

But the Lord's Prayer offers us hope. Jesus tells us to pray for today's needs—and then He tells us to rely on God's power for the future. Through Jesus, we are citizens of a kingdom that will last forever, a kingdom of light and splendor. Why should we fear the future, when—no matter what it holds—it will lead us higher and deeper into the Father's kingdom?

Future Glory

For I reckon that the sufferings
of this present time are not worthy
to be compared with the glory
which shall be revealed in us.
ROMANS 8:18

When it comes down to it, God, it's not all about me. I am guilty of being so selfish, self-centered, "me-focused" that I lose perspective of the big picture. Father God, when pain surrounds me, give me a glimpse of the glory that lies ahead. Help me regain a proper sense of perspective. Show me where You want me in Your will!

Eternal

For our light affliction, which
is but for a moment, worketh
for us a far more exceeding
and eternal weight of glory.
2 CORINTHIANS 4:17

———————

When I think about eternity, God, I realize that the time I spend on earth is pretty insignificant. But I still get so focused on my daily problems, Lord, that they seem insurmountable. Burdens and worries eat away at my joy, Lord. Instead, I choose to yield myself to whatever comes into my life and rely on Your power to get me through. Use my problems and troubles to transform me for eternity, I pray.

Blessed Hope

*Looking for that blessed hope, and
the glorious appearing of the great
God and our Saviour Jesus Christ. . .*
TITUS 2:13

———

Some days, Father, I hold on to a single thread of hope. But the hope You offer through Jesus Christ is real and active, and even when it's wearing thin, it sustains me. The hope I have in You, God, is for the future—but it blesses me today. Fortify my hope so that I can share it with other weary travelers in this world. Help me direct them to the true source of hope.

When Christ Appears

When Christ, who is our life,
shall appear, then shall ye also
appear with him in glory.
COLOSSIANS 3:4

Jesus, I look forward to Your return to earth. I'm so thankful that I am not on my own—that You are with me all the way. Thank You for the gift of Your Holy Spirit that lives in me and empowers me with the strength necessary to live for God. You are my life now, and You will take me with You into glory, where I will be made perfect.

God's Thoughts

For I know the thoughts that I
think toward you, saith the LORD,
thoughts of peace, and not of evil,
to give you an expected end.
JEREMIAH 29:11

———————

God, You know how easily my
thoughts turn to worries and fears.
Teach me to think Your thoughts
instead: thoughts of peace and
goodness that will lead me into the
future You have planned for me.
Show me the steps I should take
to reach the abundant life You have
in store for me, both here on earth
and in eternity.

Before the World Began

In hope of eternal life,
which God, that cannot lie,
promised before the world began.
TITUS 1:2

Think of it, Father! You are a God that cannot lie—there is no falsehood or deceit in You. Your promises are better than gold and they reach forward into eternity—and they reach backward, before the heavens and earth were made. There is no place in time's long arc where You are not, so why should I worry about past, present, or future? Hold me in Your hand today.

God's Riches

*O the depth of the riches both of
the wisdom and knowledge of God!
how unsearchable are his judgments,
and his ways past finding out!*
ROMANS 11:33

When I start to worry about my
life, Father, when I start to feel as
though You may not know what
You're doing—remind me that
Your riches are far greater than my
needs. Give me a spirit of peace
when I don't understand the whys,
secure in my faith that You are
doing a good work that will bring
glory to Your name.

All Grace

The God of all grace, who hath called us unto his eternal glory by Christ Jesus, after that ye have suffered a while, make you perfect, stablish, strengthen, settle you.

1 PETER 5:10

———

I'm glad, God, that Your grace is so wide and great that it can work even through this life's pain and suffering. Give me the right amount of comfort to endure those times of pain and suffering, and remind me that in the end, I can count on You to make me perfect and strong, settled in Your love forever.

Abundance

[God] is able to do exceeding abundantly above all that we ask or think, according to the power that worketh in us.

EPHESIANS 3:20

———

Father, I often put limits on what is possible in my life—to my own detriment! Help me to recall the miracles You've done in my life— the "God-incidents" that have Your fingerprints all over them. Remind me to share these fantastic stories with others so they too might learn to see You at work in their lives. Give me Your eyes to see the endless power You have at work in me. May I expect Your abundance to fill my future.

Shining More and More

The path of the just is as the shining light, that shineth more and more unto the perfect day.
PROVERBS 4:18

———

Father, when I am in vibrant fellowship with You, the path before me seems clearer and Your will seems more evident. Thank You for the light that shines brighter with each step I take. When the light seems dim or I'm not sure which way to go, bring me back into Your presence, and lead me to Your holy Word. Thank You for never giving up on me, Father.

Like Jesus

Beloved, now are we the sons of God,
and it doth not yet appear what we
shall be: but we know that, when he
shall appear, we shall be like him;
for we shall see him as he is.

1 JOHN 3:2

God, You promise that You're not done with me yet. In fact, I won't be a finished until You come again to the earth and take me home with You. It doesn't really matter what my future holds, God, so long as one day I will be like Jesus.

Face-to-Face

For now we see through a glass,
darkly; but then face to face:
now I know in part; but then shall
I know even as also I am known.

1 CORINTHIANS 13:12

———

You know that I can't see You clearly, Father. You know I don't really understand You, even when I am seeking You every day. I'm grateful, though, that I expect to see You face-to-face—and that on that day, I will finally truly know You even more intimately and personally than now. What an awe-inspiring promise!

Glory to Glory

But we all, with open face beholding
as in a glass the glory of the Lord,
are changed into the same image
from glory to glory, even as by
the Spirit of the Lord.
2 CORINTHIANS 3:18

You have given me glory in this
world, God. You have given me
splendor and light. You have created my very essence so that it
shines. And as I keep my eyes on
You, You are creating within me
even greater glory. May Your Spirit
work in my heart, God, so that I
am transformed into Your image.

Strength to Strength

They go from strength to strength.
PSALM 84:7

———————

You know the strength I need to face today, Lord. You know the strength I'll need for tomorrow, for next week, for next year. You know what I'll need to face each of the challenges that lies ahead in my life. You know the day of my death, and You know exactly what I'll need on that day, too. So I need not worry about anything. You will lead me from strength to strength, like jumping from stone to stone across a river.

With Jesus

Father, I will that they also, whom
thou hast given me, be with me
where I am; that they may behold my
glory, which thou hast given me.
JOHN 17:24

———

God, as much as I may wish I knew
what the future holds, only You
know what will happen. Instead of
worrying about things that I cannot control, I want to simply follow You into tomorrow and into
eternity. The truth is, I don't really
care where You lead me. . .so long
as Jesus is there, too.

Joy

For ye shall go out with joy, and be led forth with peace: the mountains and the hills shall break forth before you into singing, and all the trees of the field shall clap their hands.

ISAIAH 55:12

———

Some days, Lord, things are going so well that it feels like all creation is singing Your praises, and I join with them. Other days, even when creation sings, I don't feel like praising. Thank You, Lord, for the reminder from the mountains and trees that no matter what today brings, You promise me joy. Help me to live out Your joy every day.

AMEN

(Agreement in Prayer)

When we are done with praying, we automatically say the word "Amen." We often treat this small word as though it were the "good-bye" we mutter at the end of a phone conversation. We use it to say in effect, "Signing off now, God. I'm going back to my life, and I'll talk to You later."

But this ancient Hebrew word actually means something quite different. It is a way to seal the truth of what we have just prayed. It expresses our wholehearted commitment to our prayer, our total agreement. Heart, mind, and body, we surrender ourselves to God's answer to our prayer.

Let It Be

And Mary said, Behold the handmaid of the Lord; be it unto me according to thy word.

LUKE 1:38

Lord, help me to follow Mary's example when she found out that she was pregnant with the Son of God. Her world was rocked, God! What a scandal! A good Jewish girl pregnant before she was married? Unthinkable! But she accepted the news and surrendered her life and her body to Your will. Help me to accept Your word, no matter what it says to me, and surrender myself to it.

Right Motives

*Ye ask, and receive not, because ye
ask amiss, that ye may consume
it upon your lusts.*
JAMES 4:3

———————

God, I admit that sometimes I
am guilty of treating my prayers
as a wish list to a Santa-God. Or
maybe I treat You as though You
were a vending machine—if I say
the right words in the right order,
I'll get what I want. If I'm honest,
I know that selfishness and greed
may slip into a request here or
there. Today I ask that You show
me when my prayers are corrupted
by selfish desires. Give me pure
motives, a pure heart, and a clear
conscience.

Confidence

*And this is the confidence that
we have in him, that, if we ask
any thing according to his will,
he heareth us.*

1 JOHN 5:14

As I pray, Lord, I rest in the confidence that You are always listening and that You understand the thoughts behind my prayers, even when I cannot. I am never speaking into empty air! Thank You for the confidence I also experience through the power of Your Holy Spirit that lives inside my heart. With You on my side, I can accomplish much for Your kingdom!

The Truth

*Jesus saith unto him, I am the way,
the truth, and the life: no man
cometh unto the Father, but by me.*
JOHN 14:6

When I pray to You, God, I pray
in Your Son's name. He is the way,
He is the truth, and He will show
me the way to You so that I can
live the life that You intend for me.
Help me to not be distracted by
other false paths that may seem at-
tractive or easier. Make my journey
one that invites others to follow
me, just as I follow Christ.

United in Prayer

I say unto you, That if two of you shall agree on earth as touching any thing that they shall ask, it shall be done for them of my Father which is in heaven.

MATTHEW 18:19

———

Thank You, Lord, for others who share my faith in You. Thank You for the privilege of praying with them, for worshipping with them, for working together to build Your kingdom. Thank You that when we pray together, You hear us and that when we gather together, You are there with us. Help us to be the living, breathing, and active body of Christ that we are meant to be.

Abiding

If ye abide in me, and my words abide in you, ye shall ask what ye will, and it shall be done unto you.

JOHN 15:7

Father, help me to abide in You as I pray—not quickly spitting out my requests and then dwelling on my worries and woes. Keep my thoughts focused on You as I wait for Your answers to my prayers, no matter how soon You answer them. Keep me close and allow me to abide in You as You ultimately answer my requests, and give me the peace of knowing that You work all things for good.

Wavering Hearts

Let him ask in faith, nothing wavering. For he that wavereth is like a wave of the sea driven with the wind and tossed.

JAMES 1:6

———

You know how easily my heart wavers and wobbles, Lord. I'm like a boat that's out in open water, the world's woes tossing me around like high waves. Take the helm of my boat, I pray. And then after I've given over control of the boat, quiet the wind and waves. Help me to pray with faith's absolute calm, knowing that You have already ordained the outcome and that You have my best interest at heart.

Anything!

*For verily I say unto you, That
whosoever shall say unto this
mountain, Be thou removed,
and be thou cast into the sea; and
shall not doubt in his heart, but shall
believe that those things which he
saith shall come to pass; he shall
have whatsoever he saith.*

MARK 11:23

———

I don't want to throw any mountains into the ocean, God—and it's
hard for me to believe that Jesus
really meant what He said here.
Show me the truth of His words.
Teach me to pray according to
Your will.

Power

*The effectual fervent prayer of a
righteous man availeth much.*
JAMES 5:16

———

Sometimes I say, "The only thing
I can do now is pray." I mean that
I've done everything I could think
to do, and now as a last resort, I'll
fall back on prayer. Forgive me,
Father, for trusting in things that
are not from You and for setting
my mind on worldly things. Remind me that prayer is never the
last resort and that You are faithful
in hearing it. Teach me to see the
power that prayer can unleash in
the world.

In All My Ways

In all thy ways acknowledge him,
and he shall direct thy paths.
PROVERBS 3:6

God, I claim Your presence in each aspect of my life. Thank You for Your steadfast love and abounding grace. I honor You alone with my successes and acknowledge Your guiding hand on my life. Help me to set my eyes only on You. Teach me what it is to trust You with all my heart and to not lean on my own wisdom or understanding. May my heart always seek to bring glory to Your name, and may my prayers always reflect this reality.

Willing Mind

*Know thou the God of thy father,
and serve him with a perfect heart
and with a willing mind: for the
LORD searcheth all hearts, and
understandeth all the imaginations
of the thoughts: if thou seek him,
he will be found of thee.*
1 CHRONICLES 28:9

———

Make my mind willing, Lord. Help
me to trust that Your plans for me
are better than the plans I have for
myself. Place Your desires in my
heart, that I may be able to walk
fully in Your will for my life. Help
me to agree with Your ways for my
life. I seek You who understands
me completely.

Perfect Heart

*Let your heart therefore be perfect
with the LORD our God, to walk
in his statutes, and to keep his
commandments, as at this day.*
I KINGS 8:61

You know I can never achieve per-
fection on my own, Lord God.
But I surrender my heart to You
absolutely. Keep my heart and
mind from wandering, and allow
me to remain true only to You. I
thank You for Your never-ending
grace that sustains my life and that
You never leave me or forsake me.
Through my prayer, I commit myself totally to You and Your law for
my life.

Willing

I know also, my God, that thou triest the heart, and hast pleasure in uprightness. As for me, in the uprightness of mine heart I have willingly offered all these things.
1 CHRONICLES 29:17

———

I give You, God, everything I have to offer, willingly and gladly. I know that everything I have You have provided and have entrusted to me. Give me a whole heart to follow after You and keep Your commandments. Keep forever in my heart Your purposes and thoughts. Show me anything I am holding back. I want You to have it all.

Truthful Heart

LORD, who shall abide in thy
tabernacle? who shall dwell in thy
holy hill? He that walketh uprightly,
and worketh righteousness, and
speaketh the truth in his heart.
PSALM 15:1–2

Lord, sometimes I lie to myself.
Sometimes I try to lie to You. But
You know me. You know my
thoughts before I think them. Reveal to me Your truth, so that my
prayers may be true, righteous, and
upright. Show me how to live a
blameless life.

One Mind

That ye may with one mind and
one mouth glorify God, even the
Father of our Lord Jesus Christ.
ROMANS 15:6

Unite me in prayer with others, Father God. Let no division come between us as we talk with You. Give me patience in dealing with people who aren't exactly like me and can be trying; remind me that patience will build up Your church. Forgive me for any gossip or malicious words I've spoken against my brothers and sisters, and give me a heart that longs for their good. Bring to my mind ways I can show love that will bring more glory to You.

Believing

Be not faithless, but believing.
JOHN 20:27

I believe in You, Jesus. I believe in Your power and wisdom and love. I believe that Your atoning work on the cross has washed me of all my unrighteousness and that through it, I stand in perfect righteousness before God. Take my life—all my words and deeds—and use them for Your glory. Teach me to trust You, not requiring proof as Thomas did, but believing You at Your Word alone. Thank You that Your Word is truth and brings life to me and to those around me.

Scripture Index